This book is about a superhero, who at the right moment in time was rewarded for a dedicated heart. The power of THE ROSSMAN is amazing!

Text copywright 2010 by Julie Guerry
Illustration copywright 2010 by Carylon Killebrew
All rights reserved
Design and Layout by Travis Wright
The illustrations in this bookwere rendered using acrylic paint on handmade paper
Manufactured in Chattanooga, TN

The Rossman a superhero at heart : by Julie Guerry: Illustrated by Carylon Killebrew – 1st ed.
ISBN-10: 0983095302
ISBN-13: 9780983095309
1. Dogs – Childrens Literature. 2. Childrens Literature – Family
Summary: A true story about a three-legged dog who finds a loving home and realizing his
superstrenghts come from hope, courage and love.

Blueberry Press, LLC.
115 Maple Avenue, Lookout Mountain, Tennessee 37350

THE ROSSMAN

a superhero at heart

written by Julie Guerry

illustrated by Carylon Killebrew

I wasn't always the Rossman.

This is my story.

I LIVED UNDER A TRAILER,

no one noticed me.
I never had enough food.

There had to be a place that was better...

I ESCAPED.

I RAN

I ran as fast as I could.

I ran to find the good,
and a car hit me.
The car hit me with
so much **power!**

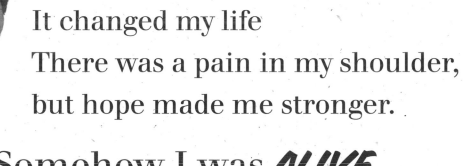

It changed my life
There was a pain in my shoulder,
but hope made me stronger.

Somehow I was *ALIVE*.

My front leg was crushed.

A doctor named Tai
started to heal me.
He wrapped my wound
in a **purple** bandage.

He told me purple was a
symbol of **courage.**
He told me I was going to have
three super legs.

Courage made me trust.
I was changing.

For three months I lived in my hospital home.

Three special girls came to visit me.

They brought me clean blankets and

homemade poundcake.

Hagan, Margaret and Helen,

came to see me often.

They needed to be with me. I began to care about living.

Hope is believing that
something or someone
is going to rescue you
and you can live happily ever after.

My family was that
someone.

When it was time to
leave the hospital,
my new mom and dad
helped remove my
purple bandage.

I felt so *ALIVE!*

They called me

THE ROSSMAN

I am their *SUPERHERO!*

My home is amazing!

My mom fills my body with good food

and she doesn't get mad when

I win the

pillow fights.

My dad recognizes my
need to protect
by letting me sleep
at the end of the bed.

My three girls
tell me they love me,
all the time.

My family takes me
on vacation to
Sea Island
I love the beach.
My dad throws me
tennis balls in the ocean,
and my mom looks for sea turtle tracks in the sand.
I watch my girls help the horseshoe crabs back to the water.

This is a good place.

Hank

Maggie

Gracie

At my home,
I live with a
dog team.
There are four of us.
We train daily to
protect our family.

We sharpen our skills with the exterminator

leaf blower

mail carrier

Our family needs us.
We will be ready.

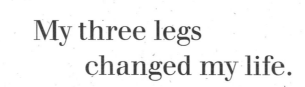

My three legs
  changed my life.

Hope gave me **STRENGTH.**

Courage made me **TRUST.**

Love gave me **LOYALTY.**

These are my **SUPERPOWERS.**

I am

THE ROSSMAN

My story does not end here....